THE ANCIENT WORLD

ANCIENT INDIA

BY ALLISON LASSIEUR

CHILDREN'S PRESS®
AN IMPRINT OF SCHOLASTIC INC.
NEW YORK   TORONTO   LONDON   AUCKLAND   SYDNEY
MEXICO CITY   NEW DELHI   HONG KONG
DANBURY, CONNECTICUT

Library of Congress Cataloging-in-Publication Data
Lassieur, Allison.
  Ancient India/by Allison Lassieur.
    p. cm.—(The Ancient world)
  Includes bibliographical references and index.
  ISBN: 978-0-531-25180-5 (lib. bdg.)
  ISBN: 978-0-531-25980-1 (pbk.)
  1. India—Civilization—To 1200—Juvenile literature. I. Title.
  DS425.L37 2013
  934—dc23   2012000508

Content Consultant
Julia Shaw, Lecturer in South Asian Archaeology, Institute of Archaeology, University College, London

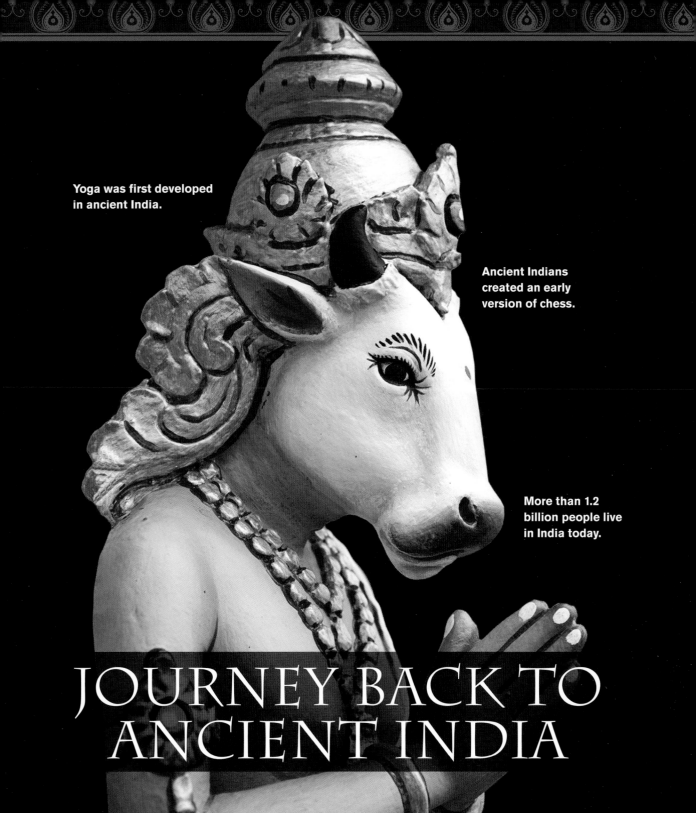

Yoga was first developed in ancient India.

Ancient Indians created an early version of chess.

More than 1.2 billion people live in India today.

JOURNEY BACK TO ANCIENT INDIA

TABLE OF CONTENTS

A seal from the ruins of Mohenjo Daro

A Gupta carving

MYSTERY OF THE FORGOTTEN CIVILIZATION

I t was a mystery without a main character. In the nineteenth century, **archaeologists** studying the ancient cultures of Egypt (ca. 3150 BCE to 30 BCE) and Sumeria (ca. 4000 BCE to

Archaeologists are careful to avoid damaging the artifacts they discover.

1940 BCE) found clues to another great **civilization** that existed alongside them. This civilization was referred to as Meluhha. It was the center of a powerful manufacturing culture. The people of Meluhha traded in copper, ceramics, and other goods. It was clear from the evidence that this culture was as large, wealthy, and powerful as Egypt and Sumeria. But was Meluhha really a newly discovered civilization? Or was "Meluhha" simply another name for a previously discovered place? No one knew.

Nineteenth-century explorers searching for the beginnings of ancient India faced a similar problem. They had already learned much about India's vibrant early civilizations from sacred religious texts. Accounts from ancient Indian kings provided them with

Archaeologists have uncovered entire buildings and settlements in India.

archaeologists (ahr-kee-AH-luh-jists) people who study the past, which often involves digging up old buildings, objects, and bones and examining them carefully

civilization (siv-uh-li-ZAY-shun) a developed and organized society

Ancient artwork provides clues about the origins of ancient Indian culture.

information about politics and battles. Early European travelers commented on temples on the southern coast of India.

These sites and writings, however, were much more recent than ancient Egyptian or Sumerian civilizations. Scholars, working with the information available, assumed that the Indian civilization developed thousands of years after Egypt or Sumeria. Some researchers estimated that time to be about the time of Buddha, who lived around 500 BCE. What archaeologists wanted desperately to find was something older, perhaps the ruins of a great city or structure. With such a find, they could confidently claim, "Here, it began. Here lie the origins of Indian civilization."

Over the years, clues, such as stone tools, had been found to help date the ancient Indian civilizations. But given the information at the time, there was nothing to suggest the existence of an urban culture that might have been as old as the Egyptian or Mesopotamian civilizations further to the west. Until the early 20th century, the origins of Indian urbanism and state formation were placed in the third century BCE, during the Mauryan period. Finally, in 1924, Sir John Marshall, a British archaeologist, published an announcement in the *Illustrated London News*. It read:

The archaeologist John Marshall made important contributions to the study of ancient India.

Not often has it been given to archaeologists . . . to light upon the remains of a long-forgotten civilization. It looks, however, at this moment, as if we were on the threshold of such a discovery on the plains of the Indus. Up to the present our knowledge of Indian antiquities has carried us back hardly further than the third century before Christ [BCE] . . . Now, however, there has unexpectedly been unearthed, in the south of the Panjab and in Sind, an entirely new class of objects which have nothing in common with those previously known to us, and which are unaccompanied by any date that might have helped us to establish their age and origin.

Marshall's dig site was near the small village of Harappa, in present-day northeastern Pakistan. There he had unearthed the remains of a large city with substantial brick structures, pottery, and other materials. The remains dated thousands of years earlier than any other urban settlement that had been found before. Marshall's team was astounded at the quality and scope of the objects. At Harappa, Marshall had found something completely unexpected: a bustling, large society that no one thought had ever existed. Was this culture of Harappa the mysterious Meluhha, the trading partner of Egypt and Sumeria? Archaeologists believed it was.

Since that discovery almost one hundred years ago, hundreds of ancient Harappan archaeological sites have been documented, revealing a large ancient culture with hundreds of villages and cities. These early Indian cultures were as advanced and powerful as their Egyptian and Sumerian neighbors, and could possibly have been even greater.

Harappa and its sister city, Mohenjo Daro, also in present-day Pakistan, are the earliest links in the long chain of what was ancient India. There is no one "ancient Indian civilization" or government or culture. Rather, the story of ancient India is the story of many civilizations that grew, became powerful, and fell. In their wake, they left behind art, religion, government, and culture that continue to be part of modern India today.

Though the ruins of Mohenjo Daro are located in Pakistan, they are a key site in understanding the roots of ancient India.

CHAPTER ONE

MANY EMPIRES, ONE INDIA

The year was 262 BCE, and the people in the small Indian kingdom of Kalinga were terrified. Ashoka, the ruthless and barbaric emperor of the Mauryan Empire, and his army approached from nearby. His goal was to destroy Kalinga, seize its resources, and add to his growing Indian empire. The

This carving, an artifact of Ashoka's reign, dates back to 238 BCE.

Kalinga people had already heard stories of Ashoka's cruelty. It was said he murdered his own brothers to capture the throne of India. Other stories claimed that he killed five hundred ministers even after they passed a loyalty test. Other sources said he built a torture chamber for his own personal amusement so he could watch his many victims die in agony.

When Ashoka attacked, however, the Kalinga people did not flee. They stood their ground with weapons, ready to defend themselves against the Mauryans' assault. Ashoka's attack was devastating. More than 100,000 people were killed, and another 150,000 were captured. When the fighting ended, Ashoka walked through the battlefield and saw the lifeless bodies of soldiers, women, and children lying in piles. He was horrified by the suffering he had caused.

Ashoka was forever changed by what he witnessed at Kalinga. He dedicated his life to Buddhism and rejected violence and war. During the rest of his rule, Ashoka announced new laws that preached nonviolence and the dignity of human beings. These laws were carved into tall stone **pillars** and rocks throughout the empire.

The ancient Mauryan Empire lasted about fifty years after Ashoka's death in 232 BCE. Over a long period of time, Ashoka was eventually forgotten everywhere except in a few ancient Buddhist texts. People also forgot how to read the stone carvings on the pillars. Then, in 1837 CE, an English architect and ancient-coin expert named James Prinsep **deciphered** the script in which the edicts were carved. Today, Ashoka's **edicts** are among the most famous ancient Indian artifacts. The edicts give modern scholars and historians a glimpse into the world of ancient India.

pillars (PIL-urz) columns that support part of a building or that stand alone as a monument

deciphered (di-SYE-fuhrd) figured out something that is written in code or is hard to understand

edicts (EE-dikts) orders issued by a person in authority

The Past Is Present
CHILL OUT!

Yoga is a Hindu physical, spiritual, and mental discipline that trains a person's mind for a state of perfect insight and inner peace. Yoga originated in India, and today it is practiced by millions of people around the world. Although its exact origins are unknown, yoga was first mentioned in Yajnavalkya's sutra, which was possibly contemporary with the late Vedic texts. Over the centuries, yoga evolved to include new forms and techniques, although trying to separate the mind from the physical world remains its primary goal. In the Western world, meditation is the most popular yoga technique. Meditating while combining breathing and posture control helps relieve stress and tension. Many people also meditate to treat pain and various illnesses.

THE FIRST PEOPLE: INDUS VALLEY CULTURE

By about 2600 BCE, a great culture existed in ancient India in the Indus Valley region. Today, archaeologists refer to the culture of that area as either the Indus Valley or Harappan civilization. The two best-known Indus Valley cities are Harappa and Mohenjo Daro, but recent **excavations** have unearthed hundreds of Indus Valley villages, towns, and cities. Mohenjo Daro and Harappa were probably the capitals.

Historians must rely on primary sources such as archaeological evidence to understand the Indus Valley culture, although not

Ashoka's pillars are still standing at many ancient Indian sites.

excavations (ek-skuh-VAY-shunz) holes dug in the earth to search for something buried, as in archaeological research

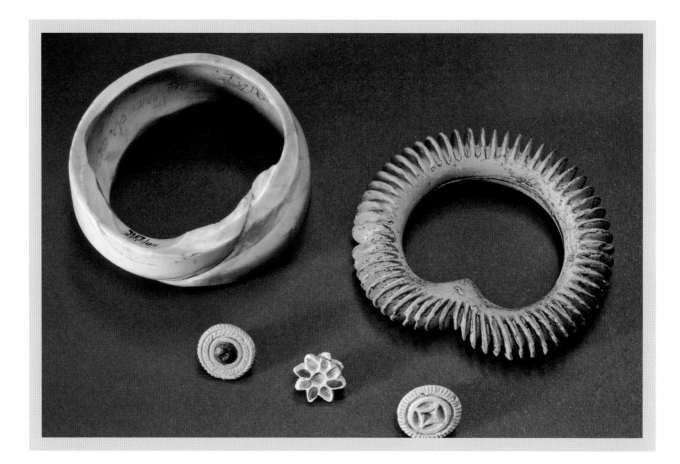

The people of the Indus Valley left behind artifacts such as these bracelets and earrings.

much evidence has survived. In fact, it is the lack of certain kinds of information that has shaped our understanding of the Indus Valley people. There is no conclusive evidence of a ruler or unified government, for instance, but the nature of the evidence has led to comparisons with contemporaneous state-level societies such as Mesopotamia or Egypt. Signs of manufacturing facilities and supplies of raw materials suggest both local and long-distance trading, but it's unknown who controlled it. There is also little evidence of the religious practices the Indus Valley cultures followed, though there is much speculation about this topic.

Sometime between 1800 BCE and 1700 BCE, the civilization in the Indus Valley faded away. Some historians believe that a decline in trade or massive floods may have contributed to its mysterious disappearance. Others think the civilization may have been invaded by enemies, although no one is certain. By about 1700 BCE, however, the civilization had largely ceased to exist.

THE PEOPLE OF THE VEDAS

The Vedas are a collection of sacred hymns, charms, spells, and observations written in the Sanskrit language. The oldest writings date back to about 1500 BCE. Filled with hymns, descriptions of religious rituals, and epic mythical battles, the Vedas provide much of what we know about ancient India prior to 500 BCE.

Without written records, archaeologists must rely on artifacts to understand how the Indus Valley people lived.

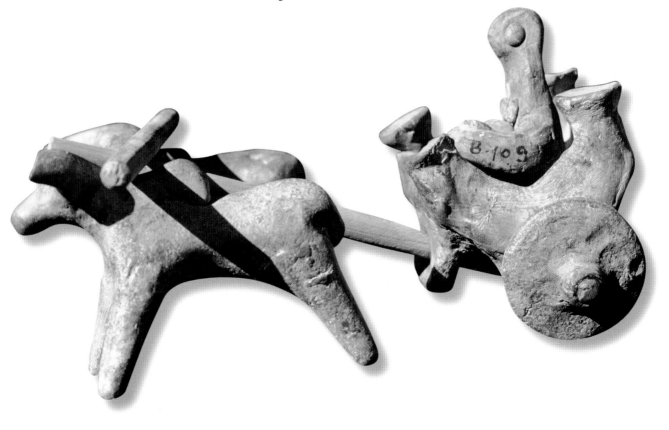

nomads (NO-madz) members of a community who travel from place to place instead of living in the same place all the time

monsoon (mahn-SOON) a rainy summer season brought on by strong winds from the ocean

clans (KLANZ) large groups of families descended from a common ancestor

monarchies (MAH-nur-keez) governments in which the head of state is a king or queen

The Vedas describe a group of **nomads** who settled in the upper reaches of the Punjab, southeast of Harappa. It is not known whether the Aryas, the political elite mentioned in the Vedas, were native to the area or whether they migrated from another region.

The people were originally herdsmen, frequently on the move as they sought new lands for their cattle to graze on. They most likely established their first temporary settlements during the heavy rains of the **monsoon** seasons. Barley was the first crop they planted and harvested.

Vedic society was organized into **clans**, or tribes, each made up of a number of related families. Hostilities between clans were common, as they often stole each other's livestock or seized grazing lands. Controlling river water was another frequent cause of unrest between tribes.

The Monarchies of the Ganges River Valley

During the later years of the Vedic society, the Indus Valley was no longer considered India's heartland. Instead, the Gangetic Plain became the focus of the developing society. For the first time, organized, well-governed towns began to spring up, ruled by newly established kingdoms and **monarchies**.

These towns developed out of the early settlements established by clans. Homes were built to be more durable than they were in the past. Mud brick was often used as the building material. Moats or walls were constructed around many towns as protection against the river's floodwaters and potential enemies. Streets were cleared and smoothed to allow wheeled vehicles to travel on them.

The development of towns relied heavily on trade, not only within the Gangetic Plain but beyond it as well. Commonly traded

The Vedas remain important religious texts for many modern Indians.

The Ganges River is about 1,560 miles (2,510 kilometers) long.

These storage jars found in the ruins of Mohenjo Daro date back to about 2500 BCE.

goods included salt beads, pottery, textiles, and iron objects such as knives, hooks, and nails.

As each town grew, it attracted newcomers from outside the family clan. No longer were all people of a settlement related or engaged in the same occupation. Metalworkers, artisans, farmers, craftsmen, and a variety of skilled people inhabited the towns. They produced a wide range of goods and services, and created an environment that incorporated different classes of people and diverse religious groups.

The emergence of towns ultimately led to the need for a centralized government that was capable of supervising the affairs of the main town and the surrounding smaller ones. Kingdoms became the most common form of government. The chiefs and local leaders of the clan system were replaced by the supreme power of a king who had the authority to enforce laws.

These copper tools date back to the Indus Valley civilization.

The king was assisted by advisers and administrators whose primary role was to collect taxes. The amount of taxes a person owed was based on the size of the land he owned and the amount of crops it produced. Traders and merchants were taxed on the amount and types of goods they bought and sold. The tax monies were used to pay the salaries of public workers, to maintain an army, and to undertake projects that would benefit the state, such as building roads or irrigation systems. Tax money was also given to priests and to members of the ruling family.

As power became concentrated in the hands of the kings and their families, strict divisions within society began to form. In the days of Vedic clan dominance, there was only minor social distinction between members of the clan. In the kingdoms and monarchies of the Gangetic Plain, however, the differences between the king and his subjects, and the rich and the poor, were vast. The centralized government of kingdoms had created a system of power and wealth at the top, supported by a peasant economy at the bottom.

INVADERS FROM THE WEST

By the sixth century BCE, northwestern India was under the control of the Achaemenid Empire of Persia, present-day Iran. The vast Persian Empire stretched from North Africa and Egypt in the west across southwestern Asia as far east as the Indus River.

The Persians, however, weren't the only military superpower with dreams of regional conquest. In 333 BCE, Alexander III (also known as Alexander the Great) of Macedon, in present-day Greece, began a series of campaigns that ultimately toppled the Persian Empire. In 326 BCE, Alexander marched on the northwestern provinces of India. The fighting lasted about two years and ended when Alexander's soldiers, weary from the constant, hard-fought battles with the Indians, refused to fight any longer.

Alexander placed several governors to rule over the Indian territories he had conquered before withdrawing from the northwest. Upon Alexander's death shortly after he left the region, however, the governors left India.

Alexander's campaign in northwestern India seemed to have little political or military influence on Indian culture. Although early Indian writings don't say much about Alexander, many Greeks marching with him recorded detailed descriptions of the

Alexander the Great and his army defeated the Persians at the Battle of the Granicus in 334 BCE.

Indian land and its people. Their impressions offer a glimpse into early Indian life, and include insightful accounts of Indian customs, clothing, and local politics.

dynasty (DYE-nuh-stee) series of rulers belonging to the same family

alliances (uh-LYE-uhn-sez) agreements to work together for some result

THE RISE OF THE MAURYAN EMPIRE

In 321 BCE, an ambitious young man named Chandragupta Maurya seized the throne of the short-lived Nanda **dynasty** with a combination of successful military campaigns and powerful political **alliances**. By the time Chandragupta stepped down from power in 297 BCE, the Mauryan Empire extended much farther than it had before. Chandragupta was succeeded by his son, Bindusara, of whom little is known, although he did extend the reach of the empire.

The Indian ruler Porus surrendered to Alexander in 326 BCE.

missionaries (MISH-uh-ner-eez) people who are sent to a foreign land to teach about religion

In 270 BCE, Bindusara's son Ashoka assumed the throne. Ashoka had earlier gained valuable political and administrative experience, having served as a governor in one of the territories under Mauryan control.

Much of what we know about Ashoka's reign and his policies come from the Rock Edicts and Pillar Edicts that he had inscribed and placed throughout the empire. Ashoka spoke directly to his subjects through the edicts, communicating his beliefs and accomplishments in a personal and direct way. The Rock Edicts were carvings on rocks situated near permanent settlements and heavily populated areas. The giant Pillar Edicts were placed on the Gangetic Plain, the center of the Mauryan Empire. They are also found in central India and the Nepalese terai.

Ashoka's reign was marked by two major events: the Battle of Kalinga and the growth of Buddhism. The destruction and loss of life at Kalinga filled Ashoka with horror and sadness. In time, he came to embrace the teachings of Buddhism and to promote nonviolence. Encouraged by their king's devotion to Buddhism, **missionaries** traveled to all corners of the Mauryan Empire—and far beyond—to preach and bring newcomers to their religion. Today, there are between 350 million and 500 million Buddhists worldwide.

Shortly after Ashoka's death in 232 BCE, the Mauryan Empire began to crumble. Although the empire's influence declined, India was not thrown into a period of political upheaval. The larger regions of India slowly transformed into independent states, where dynasties occasionally ruled.

For the next several centuries, India was without a single, dominant political force. This was to change, however, with the rise of the Gupta culture in the fourth century CE.

Thanks to their carefully etched inscriptions, many of Ashoka's Rock Edicts are still readable today.

Buddhist artwork can be found at many holy sites in modern India.

THE RISE OF THE GUPTAS

In about 320 CE, a new dynasty began to emerge in northern India. Chandragupta I, ruler of several small states, married into another powerful family and established even firmer authority throughout the Ganges region. In 335 CE, he was succeeded by his son Samudragupta, whose goal was to establish a vast empire, like the Mauryans. Samudragupta conquered and seized the territories of several local kings in the north. In other regions, he forced local

This statue of Buddha dates back to the Gupta period.

tribute (TRIB-yoot) something done, given, or said to show thanks or respect, or to repay an obligation

rulers to pay **tribute**, rather than taking control of their lands. His political power, however, was mainly limited to the Gangetic Plain. Others controlled western India and territories in the northwest.

In about 376 CE, ruler Chandragupta II, Samudragupta's son, assumed leadership of the Guptas. Chandragupta led a victorious military campaign against the Shakas, the ruling family in western India. After taking control of the western region, the Gupta dynasty continued to grow. Eventually the Gupta Empire included smaller kingdoms in the east, all territories north to present-day Nepal, and the entire Indus Valley region to the west.

The Gupta period is often referred to as the golden age of Indian history. It was marked by outstanding accomplishments in art and architecture, literature, and philosophy. With their great wealth, the Guptas built hospitals, universities, and many notable cities.

By the early fifth century, however, the Guptas began to fear an invasion from the northwest. A large group of nomadic peoples called the White Huns had occupied central Asia and were threatening to march southward into Gupta territories.

At first, the Guptas were able to fight off the Huns, but each new invasion weakened the Gupta kingdom. In about 460 CE, Skandagupta led a spirited defense of the kingdom, but after his death in about 467 CE, the central leadership of the Guptas crumbled. Many lesser Gupta kings followed, but they had little success holding back the Huns, who finally smashed through into northern India in about 480 CE.

In 550 CE, the last Gupta ruler, Vishnugupta, died. Smaller regional kingdoms once again controlled India. The great Gupta Empire was gone, along with the powerful ancient Indian civilization.

The Guptas created a wide range of beautiful artwork, some of which survives today.

CHAPTER TWO

RULING ANCIENT INDIA

One of the passages that appears on Ashoka's Rock Edict offers an insightful look at how the Mauryan king governed his people:

> The hearing of petitions and the administration of justice have been left to the Rajjukas [government officials] so that they can do their duties unperturbed, fearlessly and confidently. It is my desire that there should be uniformity in law and uniformity in sentencing. I even go this far, to grant a three-day stay for those in prison who have been tried and sentenced to death. During this time their relatives can make appeals to have the prisoners' lives spared. If there is none to appeal on their behalf, the prisoners can give gifts in order to make merit for the next world, or observe fasts. Indeed, it is my wish that in this way, even if a prisoner's time is limited, he can prepare for the next world, and that people's self-control and generosity may grow.

Ashoka was the only ancient Indian king who recorded how he ruled his government. Information about how any other ancient Indian culture ruled and governed its people is almost nonexistent today. Yet each major culture must have had some kind of organization. The small fragments of understanding we

do have come from piecing together bits of archaeology, literature, religious texts, and the writings of other cultures. It's not
until the later eras of the Mauryans and the Guptas that we gain
a better understanding of political leaders and how governments
functioned.

The ruins of Harappa tell us very little about the government system of the Indus Valley people.

WHO RULED THE INDUS VALLEY?

One of the lingering mysteries of the early Indus Valley civilization
is how people organized and governed themselves. Even the two
largest and highly excavated sites, Harappa and Mohenjo Daro,

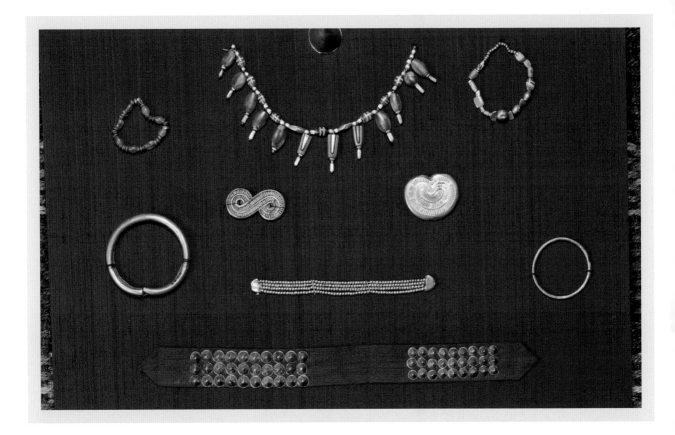

Gold jewelry has been discovered at some Indus Valley sites.

offer few clues. There are no ruins of large palaces, royal residences, or government buildings. No royal grave or tomb and no evidence of any ruler have ever been found.

But there are other clues that make a convincing case for a strong, organized system of government in the Indus Valley. The ruined city structures are laid out in a grid, meaning someone planned and organized the cities' construction. Precious copper objects and jewelry made of gold and silver have been found in some places. Some of the larger homes include a small cubicle where a guard may have stood, protecting the wealthy family who lived there. Large manufacturing areas that produced ceramics and copper have also been discovered. These point to an economy that relied on trade, which must have been controlled by someone or some group.

The Past Is Present
LET THE GAME BEGIN!

The popular game of chess originated in India during the sixth-century years of the Gupta Empire. Known as *caturanga*, meaning "four divisions," the game was played to work out military strategy. Four players used dice, four figures, and four pawns, which symbolized the four corps of the army: infantry, cavalry, chariotry, and elephantry. The four pieces became the modern pawn, knight, rook, and bishop. The game was played on special boards, or tables that were inlaid with precious jewels or woods. Young royal officers or noblemen met several times during the day to play the game.

This portion of the Mohenjo Daro ruins is believed to have been part of a market area.

Some historians believe that the rulers of Harappa and Mohenjo Daro may have lived outside of the city, in a location that has not yet been discovered. Perhaps the city leaders were priests or religious figures rather than kings. Cities may even have been governed by a group of citizens, such as an assembly or council, rather than by a single person.

These seals and sealings from Mohenjo Daro date to between 2500 and 2000 BCE. The script carved on them has yet to be deciphered.

TRIBAL LORDS OF THE VEDIC

When the Indus Valley cultures declined, so did their system of government. The society mentioned in the Vedas, who replaced them, were a nomadic, pastoral people. Their clans were called **vish**. Although the Vedas provide accounts about wars and conflicts between the clans, little is said about how the clans were organized or governed. We do know that each clan had a leader or chieftain called a **raja**. His main job was to protect his people and lead them

vish (VISH) Vedic clans or tribes

raja (RAH-jhah) a Vedic clan chieftain

This carving, found atop one of Ashoka's pillars, dates back to the Mauryan Empire.

to victory in war. He was also in charge of protecting the clan's cattle. The raja had a royal priest who went with him into battle and offered prayers to the gods. The raja was the supreme head of the government, assisted by a council made up of several officials whom he appointed. The members of the council could give advice to the raja, but final decisions were left to the raja.

Eventually, sixteen large kingdoms rose to control most of northern ancient India. Kingships in these states were passed down from father to son.

THE MAURYANS

Chandragupta's Mauryan Empire may have covered much of the Indian **subcontinent**. Millions of people lived there. To manage such a huge empire, Chandragupta established a complex network of military and government officials who helped manage the huge empire with remarkable organization and efficiency.

The network was structured in layers, beginning with Chandragupta himself. The king consulted a council of ministers that included high priests and civil officials. Beneath them were administrative departments that were in charge of various duties of the empire. These activities included collecting taxes, managing trade and commerce, running the military, maintaining cities and public places, overseeing road and irrigation projects, and maintaining markets and temples.

Chandragupta's empire was divided into four provinces, each run by someone in the royal family. That individual supervised locally appointed officials, called rajjukas, in the towns and villages. Every five years, the emperor sent officials to the provinces to determine how efficiently they were operating. This structure

subcontinent (sub-KAHN-tuh-nuhnt) a large landmass, such as India, that is part of a continent but is considered geographically or politically an independent region

The Guptas carved intricate designs into their buildings.

worked so well that most people throughout the empire with a skilled job had a supervisor they reported to. The supervisor, in turn, reported to someone higher up, and so on, all the way to the emperor himself. Some regions were better organized than others, however, and some areas were under tighter control.

The use of secret agents was another important part of the Mauryan government. The emperor established a sophisticated network of spies who posed as ordinary citizens in towns and cities throughout the empire. These royal secret agents could contact the king at any time, and they regularly brought him reports about developments in the far reaches of the kingdom. The emperor used this information to learn what his subjects thought of him, discover corrupt officials, and get military information about possible enemy attacks.

THE GUPTAS

The Gupta Empire, like the Mauryan system, was ruled by an emperor or king who had a council of ministers advising him on governmental matters. The empire was also divided into provinces, called *deshas* or *bhuktis*. A governor, or *kumaramatya*, controlled each province. The king appointed the kumaramatya, who then appointed local officials in the various districts.

Small villages were organized around a leader and a group of village elders. A council of local leaders representing merchants, artists, civil officials, and **scribes** governed larger cities. One important difference between the Mauryans and the Guptas was that the Gupta kings left their regional governments to rule as they wanted.

scribes (SKRIBZ) people who copy books, letters, contracts, and other documents by hand

CHAPTER THREE

ONE PLACE, MANY LANDS

Among the Vedas, there is a hymn dedicated to the earth goddess. The hymn praises the goddess and describes the bountiful land of India:

The earth that has heights, and slopes, and great plains, that supports the plants of manifold [many kinds of] virtue, free from the pressure that comes from the midst of men, she shall spread out for us, and fit herself for us! The earth upon which the sea, and the rivers and the waters, upon which food and the tribes of men have arisen, upon which this breathing, moving life exists, shall afford us precedence in drinking. The earth whose are the four regions of space upon which food and the tribes of men have arisen, which supports the manifold breathing, moving things, shall afford us cattle and other possessions also . . . Thy snowy mountain heights, and thy forests, O earth, shall be kind to us! The brown, the black, the red, the multi-colored, the firm earth, that is protected by Indra [the king of the gods in Hindu mythology], I have settled upon, not suppressed, not slain, not wounded.

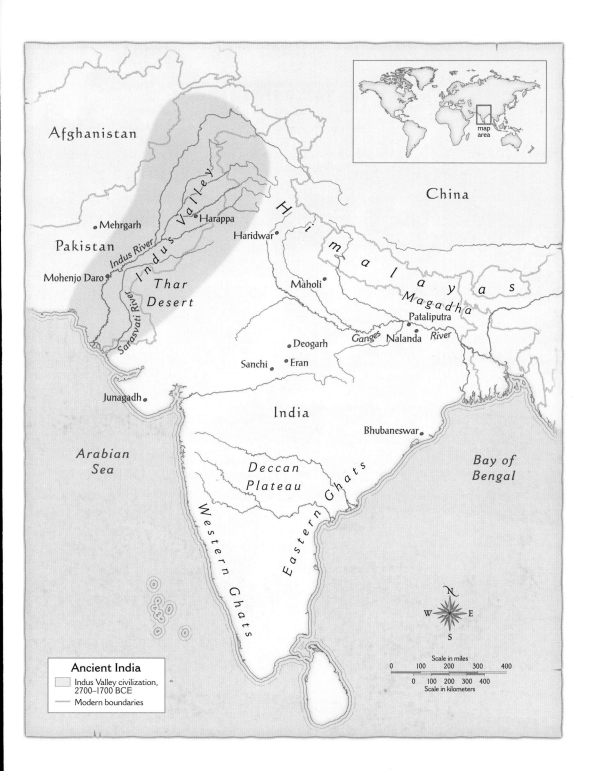

Afghanistan

China

Pakistan

Mehrgarh

Indus River

Indus Valley

Harappa

Haridwar

Himalayas

Mohenjo Daro

Thar
Desert

Maholi

Magadha

Pataliputra

Ganges

Nalanda

River

Saraswati River

Deogarh

Sanchi   Eran

Junagadh

India

Bhubaneswar

Arabian
Sea

Deccan
Plateau

Eastern Ghats

Bay of
Bengal

Western Ghats

map
area

N
W   E
S

Scale in miles
0   100   200   300   400

0   100   200 300 400
Scale in kilometers

Ancient India

Indus Valley civilization,
2700–1700 BCE

Modern boundaries

The Past Is Present
GOOD WITH NUMBERS

Although the numbers we use today are called Arabic numerals, the number system actually came from the early Hindus of ancient India. The system was passed to the Arab world and then made its way to Europe in the Middle Ages. It has changed greatly over the centuries (as shown in the diagram below), but the original system based on place value and the decimal is similar to the Hindu system. In today's system, the placement of a numeral in a number is important. In the number 259, for example, we know the "2" represents 200, the "5" represents 50, and the "9" represents 9. Our decimal system, based on increases of 10, uses ten numerals: 1 through 9 and 0. The decimal system works because of the 0, another contribution by the ancient Indians to our number system.

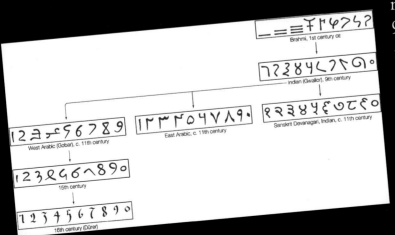

The peoples of ancient India were keenly aware that they lived in a vast and varied landscape. Nearly every type of landform and climate was found on the Indian subcontinent, from the world's highest mountain ranges in the north, to the blistering heat of the Thar Desert in the northwest, and finally to forests, lake countries, and fertile shorelines.

The geography of ancient India can be broken down into three primary areas: the mountains in the north, the sprawling plain of the Indus and Ganges rivers, and the southern peninsula.

The Himalayas prevented the people of ancient India from traveling easily to certain parts of Asia.

MOUNTAINS IN THE NORTH

The northern plain of India faces three mountain ranges to the northwest: the Hindu Kush, the Sulaiman, and the Kirthar. The passes in the northwestern mountains allowed for contact with peoples living in present-day central Asia, Iran, and Afghanistan. The climate in the mountain passes was arid, permitting easy travel and transportation of goods.

Directly north and to the northeast of the plain lie the Himalaya Mountains, also called the Himalayas. The snow-covered passes of the tall Himalayas discouraged extensive communication with the parts of Asia located across the range. Researchers, however, know for certain that a limited amount of trade was made through them. To those who follow Hinduism, the Himalayas represented the **immortality** of the divine power and the source of all life in India. The frozen, seemingly impassible, Himalaya range stretches east to west more than 1,500 miles (2,414 km). In some places, the range is 250 miles (402 km) wide. Most of the tallest mountains in the world, including Mount Everest, are part of the Himalayas.

Many of the world's major rivers, including the Ganges and Indus rivers, originate in the Himalayas. The Ganges rises in the western Himalayas and flows south and east through the Gangetic Plain, eventually emptying into the Bay of Bengal. It is 1,569 miles (2,525 km) long. The Ganges River is the most sacred river in India. It is, for most Indians, the symbol of all the sacred waters in the Hindu faith and is believed to have healing properties. Vishnu, a powerful Hindu god, is said to have bathed in the Ganges at a place called Haridwar. Today, Haridwar is so holy that bathing there can wash away even a person's more serious sins.

The 1,980-mile-long (3,186 km) Indus River rises in the

Himalayas, flows north, and then flows southwest to enter India's northern plain. Although the largest portion of the river is in present-day Pakistan, the Indus was an important natural resource and the site of major cultural developments in ancient India.

The very arid hills to the west of the Indus River valley were home to Mehrgarh, one of the earliest and most important archaeological sites in the region, dating back to about 7000 BCE. Mehrgarh is believed to be the oldest known farming settlement in South Asia. The people grew wheat and barley, and raised animals such as cattle, sheep, and goats. Artisans made beads and traded copper objects.

The Indus River was one of ancient India's most important geographical features.

Harappa and Mohenjo Daro, which thrived thousands of years later, also developed along the Indus Valley, with Harappa to the northeast of Mehrgarh and Mohenjo Daro to the southeast.

As the political and cultural focus shifted away from the Indus Valley to the Gangetic Valley, monarchies began to emerge around

Rice is a common crop in Bangladesh.

the Ganges River. There, Magadha developed as one of the leading kingdoms in the region, becoming a major political and cultural center in ancient India.

THE PLAIN OF THE INDUS AND GANGES

The northern plain is a large, fertile belt of land that covers most of northern and eastern India, parts of Pakistan and Nepal, and most of Bangladesh. The Indus forms the western portion of the plain, and the Ganges the eastern portion. The plain is fed by the waters of the rivers as well as seasonal monsoons, making the region ideal for agriculture. In ancient times, rice, wheat, and barley were commonly harvested crops. Today, sugarcane, cotton, and maize, a type of corn, are grown in abundance. However, rice is still the region's most widely-grown crop.

THE SOUTHERN PENINSULA

The peninsula in the southernmost part of the subcontinent is mainly a plateau. It is bounded by the hilly regions of the Western Ghats on the west coast and the Eastern Ghats on the east coast. The Deccan is the plateau in the northern portion of the peninsula. In ancient times, an important trade route passed through the Deccan, taking travelers and traders into the southernmost reaches of India.

The Western Ghats run about 1,000 miles (1,600 km) from the present-day state of Gujarat to the southern tip of India. Many passes through the mountains connected the inner plateau with ports on the west coast. The Western Ghats feed several rivers that run to the east and to the west, which allowed for transport

The Deccan Plateau was once the site of an important trade route.

of goods to the Bay of Bengal and the Arabian Sea. The southern portion of the Western Ghats has a humid and tropical climate, but moving north the climate becomes more temperate.

Much of the rainfall in the Western Ghats comes during winter storms. During the summer monsoon season, the high mountains force eastward-moving rain clouds to rise and drop their precipitation on the western side of the Ghats. The eastern region receives less rainfall. Rainfall in the north is often heavy but followed by long dry spells. Some regions close to the equator have rainfalls that last most of the year.

The Eastern Ghats begin in the north in the state of West Bengal and continue south in a broken line to the tip of India. Several major rivers cut through the region, once again allowing for efficient transport of people and goods. The northern hills have a cooler and much wetter climate than the nearby plains and are home to large areas of forestland. The ruins of many Buddhist sites have been found in the Eastern Ghats, some dating back to the third century BCE.

Lying between the Western and Eastern Ghats is the Deccan Plateau. The Gangetic Plain lies to the north. The Deccan generally receives little rainfall because of the tall Western Ghats that block clouds during the summer monsoon months. The climate is generally arid in the north and tropical farther south, with wet and dry seasons. Several rivers run through the region, usually flowing south.

In ancient times, the Deccan served as home to farming villages dating back to 2600 BCE. Settlements of herders, or cattle keepers, have been discovered, revealing crude dwellings and handmade pottery. Over time, these villages expanded into more advanced settlements, which came under Mauryan influence.

The peaks of the Western Ghats reach heights of 3,000 to 5,000 feet (900 to 1,500 meters).

CHAPTER FOUR

PRIESTS, FARMERS, TRADERS, AND ARTISTS

L ife in ancient India depended largely on when and where a person lived. The people of the Indus Valley culture, for instance, knew a vastly different kind of life than those of

The buildings of Mohenjo Daro had thick brick walls.

This illustration imagines what Mohenjo Daro might have looked like at its height.

the Vedic culture. An artisan living in the Mauryan Empire would be unrecognizable to artists from the Gupta Empire. Most of what is known about the lives of people from these cultures comes from archaeology and a few written texts. By piecing together these scattered clues, a picture of life throughout all the major ancient Indian civilizations emerges.

LIFE IN THE INDUS VALLEY

A person who lived in a large city such as Harappa or Mohenjo Daro enjoyed a fairly comfortable life. Most people lived in mud brick houses that lined the streets of the city. The thick walls made the inside cool and comfortable, and kept heat in during the colder months. Houses consisted of a series of rooms arranged around a small courtyard. Doorways and windows faced the quieter side lanes to keep out the street noise. Some houses had more than one floor, perhaps for more sleeping areas or storage. Doorways were covered with colorfully painted wood or reed mats. Wealthier people had large homes with many rooms joined by passageways, and sometimes other smaller rooms that might have been used by guards or servants.

Based on the ruins at Harappa and Mohenjo Daro, archaeologists can make an educated guess about how the Indus Valley people built their homes.

KEEPING IT CLEAN

Mohenjo Daro, a thriving Indus River valley city, had an advanced system of waste removal that evolved into modern sanitation technology. Most houses were constructed with connections to open channels, or sewers, in the center of the city's streets. The channels were probably covered with bricks or stones. Rather than letting the wastewater flow directly into

the channels, however, it was passed through clay pipes into a small pit. The solids settled to the bottom of the pit, while the liquids overflowed into the channels in the street. The channels also served as an effective drainage system during periods of heavy rainfall. The channels were regularly cleaned and maintained by city workers.

Archaeologists have discovered public bath areas at Mohenjo Daro.

The city people of Harappa and Mohenjo Daro also had something that no other ancient civilization of the time had: indoor plumbing and toilets. Interestingly, many modern homes in India lack these features even today. Houses, or groups of houses, had separate bathing areas in rooms next to a well. People stood on small platforms with a drain underneath and tipped water over themselves from a jar. The water fell into the drain, which was connected to a larger drain in the nearby street. Almost every house had its own toilet, which was made of large pots sunk into the floor. The waste fell through a small hole in the bottom of the pot that led into a drain. People "flushed" these toilets by pouring water into them.

Only a small percentage of the total population lived in cities. They were probably priests, merchants, artisans, and other skilled workers. Throughout the city, potters, metalworkers, brick makers, shell workers, bead makers, weavers, and jewelry makers operated small shops. The people dressed in lightweight clothing made of cotton or linen, depending on their wealth. Lower-class workers probably wore only rough leggings or **loincloths**, while wealthier men wore fine tunics. Women wore lightweight dresses, and everyone wore jewelry made of copper and beads.

loincloths (LOYN-klawths) garments worn around a man's waist

Sculptures such as this one, discovered at Harappa, indicate that Indus Valley people used animals to pull carts.

Indus Valley artisans often worked with terra-cotta, a type of clay-based ceramic.

About 90 percent of people living in the Indus Valley resided in the country. Most people farmed or tended animals, such as cattle, sheep, and goats. Farmers lived in small villages and grew a variety of crops such as wheat, barley, rice, grapes, watermelons, peas, dates, and garlic. Homes were simple structures, usually circular huts made of wooden posts with mud walls.

VEDIC LIFE

Very little is known about the daily lives of the people who are described in the Vedas. Yet the Vedas mention many occupations in which the people engaged. These included warriors, priests, cattle keepers, farmers, hunters, barbers, carpenters, metalworkers, tanners, and weavers. Other people made wine, chariots, bows and bowstrings, and mats. The people traded with each other for the things they needed, and cattle was especially valuable. Some clans had slaves, usually captured as prisoners of war.

When people gathered for a meal, they usually met at the *yagna*, or central fireplace. Mealtimes were social events where family members ate with the rest of the clan. Meat, milk products, grains, vegetables, and fruits were common foods of the Vedic diet. The people drank a beverage called soma, which was the juice taken from the stalks of the soma plant. The juice was filtered through sheep's wool and then mixed with water and milk. The people described in the Vedas believed that drinking soma made them immortal.

The people mentioned in the Vedas wore simple clothing made of animal skins or woven from cotton, wool, or goat hair. They frequently wore beaded jewelry and necklaces. At social gatherings, they sang, danced, and played musical instruments such as the flute, lute, and drums. Some people liked to gamble with dice and bet on chariot races.

Until recently, there was almost no archaeological information about the Vedic people and their daily lives. Several digs, however, have unearthed villages that might be ancient Vedic settlements. These settlements stretch along an area of India in the Thar Desert where an ancient river, the Sarasvati, once flowed. To the

The Thar Desert covers about 77,000 square miles (200,000 sq km).

Vedics, the Sarasvati was to be honored as "the best mother, the best river, the best goddess." The river is mentioned dozens of times in the Vedas as a place where battles were fought and where some tribes and clans settled. The Vedas even describe how the river eventually dried up and disappeared. But for years, many scholars had claimed that the Sarasvati was a mythical river that was simply a symbol of a goddess.

Modern technology, however, has shed new light on the mystery of the Sarasvati. In the 1970s, satellite imagery revealed an enormous dry riverbed in India located in the area where the Vedas claimed the Sarasvati flowed. To the amazement of many archaeologists, the imagery also showed that hundreds of archaeological sites dating to the Indus Valley era were built along the ancient riverbed. This indicates that the people built their villages before the Sarasvati River dried up in about 2000 BCE. If true, it could mean that the Vedas are much older than previously thought.

The Hindu goddess Sarasvati is closely associated with the river that shares her name.

LIFE IN THE MAURYAN COURT

Sometime in the fourth century BCE, a Greek statesman named Megasthenes visited the royal court of Chandragupta Maurya. Megasthenes's descriptions of the Mauryans appear in his book called *Indica* and are the first Western accounts of ancient India.

Megasthenes describes the royal city of Pataliputra (modern-day Patna in northwestern India) as the largest in India and especially lavish. The city sat on a narrow strip of land along the Ganges River, stretching about 9 miles (14.5 km) long and about 1.5 miles (2.4 km) wide. The city was surrounded by an enormous wooden wall with cutouts for archers and a deep, wide moat. There were 570 watchtowers and 64 gates, each with its own bridge or built-up roadway that crossed the moat.

According to Megasthenes, the royal family enjoyed wearing "finery and ornament." They wore robes laced in gold and decorated with precious stones. Their garments were made of fine muslin, a loosely woven cotton fabric that originated in present-day Bangladesh. Attendants walking behind the royals shielded them with umbrellas, "for they have a high regard for beauty and avail [use] themselves of every device to improve their looks."

Megasthenes observed that the royals were greatly concerned about the safety of their king. The emperor was not allowed to sleep during the day, and at night he had to change the couch he slept on from time to time "with a view to defeat plots against his life."

The king left his palace—which was surrounded by beautiful parks and gardens—to conduct war, oversee court cases, offer sacrifices to Indian gods, and go hunting. A royal Mauryan hunt was an important and elaborately planned event. Crowds of women surrounded the king as he walked down a road to the hunt.

The modern city of Patna sits upon the site of Pataliputra.

Hundreds of men with spears accompanied him, and men with drums and gongs led the march. When hunting in the open, the king sat atop an elephant shooting arrows at his target. Women riding in chariots or on horses or elephants, armed with weapons of all types, also participated.

Not all of Megasthenes's accounts provide us with accurate observations of ancient India. In one instance, he describes a race of people whose feet are turned backward and have eight toes on each foot! Another race of people supposedly had no mouths and

The ancient Indians used elephants as a form of transportation.

did not eat or drink. They were able to exist simply by smelling roots, flowers, and wild apples!

THE DAILY LIFE OF A MAURYAN EMPEROR

Kautilya was a Hindu scholar and philosopher who served as Chandragupta Maurya's chief minister. During the emperor's reign, Kautilya wrote a book entitled *Arthashastra*, which is a guide on law, government, and conducting war. The book clearly outlines the political structure of the Mauryan Empire at the time, and most of what we know today about Mauryan government comes from *Arthashastra*. However, recent scholarship shows that the text was probably composed at least 500 years later, although it may have drawn on elements of Mauryan statecraft.

Kautilya carefully describes how the palace should have multiple secret passageways and emergency exits, but it also offers suggestions on what the king should eat and drink, and the types of guards and ministers he should trust. Kautilya even goes on to plan a daily schedule for the king. His recommendations include:

1. Receive reports on defense and accounts of income and expenses.
2. Look into the affairs of the people of the cities and countryside.
3. Bathe, eat a meal, and study.
4. Assign tasks to the heads of departments.
5. Consult ministers and receive secret information brought in by spies.
6. Relax and enjoy himself.
7. Review the armies: elephants, horses, chariots, and troops.
8. Discuss military policy with commander in chief.

In the evening, Kautilya suggests the king once again interview secret agents and take another bath. He also suggests about four and a half hours of sleep each night, followed by meeting again with counselors, receiving blessings from priests, and visiting with his doctor and chief cook.

LIVING IN A GOLDEN AGE

Although the Gupta Empire lasted for only about two hundred years, many scholars believe it was the height of ancient Indian culture and art. A stable government allowed the culture to flourish and grow in ways that no other ancient Indian culture had before. Daily life was happy and comfortable for most, and quite luxurious for the wealthiest people. Most people lived in small villages and towns, and worked the land as farmers, hunters, and herdsmen. Village homes had one room and were built of bamboo or wood. Wealthier people often lived in wooden homes with several rooms.

The main areas of town were noisy and lively, with shops and merchant stalls lining the streets. Craftspeople had workshops where they made clothing, jewelry, iron, copper, carts, and other items needed for everyday use. At certain times of the year, villages joined together for large celebrations filled with dancing, music, and fine food.

Villages were generally safe places to live, because the emperor assigned a separate military squad to protect each village. Each squad included one elephant, one chariot, three armored cavalrymen, and five soldiers.

People wore clothing that was suited for the climate they lived in. In the cooler north, they wore heavier clothing than they did in the tropical southern areas. Men and women in the north wore a garment called a dhoti, a long cloth draped around the legs and tied around the waist. Dhotis were made of bright silks, cottons, or wool, depending on the person's wealth.

People commonly wore jewelry, such as armbands, bangles, ankle bracelets, rings on their toes and fingers, and elaborate hair ornaments made of rare woods and precious metals. Women carried umbrellas to protect their skin from the sun and heat, and wore white leather shoes with thick soles to make them look taller.

People in the southern areas dressed in saris, which were lighter-weight versions of the dhoti. Saris covered more of the body and were made of lighter fabrics such as cotton. They were often dyed in bright colors.

Many women continue to wear saris today.

CHAPTER FIVE

FAITH AND BEAUTY

Ancient India is not simply the story of many different empires. It is the story of how each empire made great contributions to the world in art, music, literature, religion,

People have practiced Hinduism for thousands of years.

More than a billion people practice Hinduism today.

and architecture. Each era of ancient Indian history added to the contributions made by previous ones. Perhaps the most powerful—and enduring—achievements of the ancient Indians are their religions. These ancient faiths changed and grew to become the major religions practiced in India and throughout the world today.

HINDUISM

With roughly one billion followers worldwide, Hinduism is the world's third-largest religion, following Christianity and Islam. Yet Hinduism is not exactly a religion in the Western sense. There is not a single founder of Hinduism, nor is there a single holy book that provides a history of the belief and guidelines for living. Hinduism is a cultural way of life, continually changing, that incorporates different spiritual thinking as a path to God and understanding.

The Past Is Present
COMBAT!

Some of the fighting moves shown in modern movies may have their origins in ancient India. Sanskrit epic poems such as the *Ramayana* and the *Mahabharata* describe ancient battles between figures from Hindu culture. The texts describe how warriors clashed using kicks and head–butts, and striking with the knees and elbows. Accounts of boxing matches are also vividly depicted in the writings. Some Indian fighting styles even borrowed movements from yoga and Indian dance. *Varma kalai* is an ancient fighting form that is still practiced today. It teaches how to strike dozens of points on the body that can disable or even cause the death of the victim. Today, students of this somewhat secretive **martial art** must show an understanding of many subjects, including biology, chemistry, astronomy, mathematics, yoga, and Hindu philosophies.

In addition to having its roots in ancient Indian culture, Hinduism also traces its origins to the geography of India. The word *Hindu* comes from the Sanskrit word *Sindhu*, which was an ancient name for the Indus River. The term *Hinduism* made its way into the English language as late as the nineteenth century as a word to describe the philosophies and cultural traditions with origins in ancient India.

Today, Hinduism is practiced by about 80 percent of the people in India and is thought to be "timeless," having always existed. As it developed throughout ancient Indian history, it incorporated hundreds of different beliefs, gods and goddesses,

martial art (MAHR-shuhl AHRT) style of fighting or self-defense

There are many different types of Hinduism, each with its own unique beliefs and practices.

Hindus recite hymns from the Vedas at many different ceremonies and rituals.

and guidelines for a spiritual life. Tracing Hinduism's early development is difficult because there is little information about the nature of Harappan religion, and modern Hinduism did not come together until the Gupta era.

Although Hinduism has evolved over many centuries, the ancient Vedas—hymns, instructions, and stories about Indian gods—are considered the core of Hindu scriptures, and many verses are still used as Hindu prayer today. Created by Sanskrit-speaking people around 1500 BCE, the Vedas were sung or recited until they were written down in about 300 BCE. There are four Vedas: Rig Veda, Sama Veda, Yajur Veda, and Atharva Veda. The Rig Veda was probably the earliest and is the oldest document written in the ancient language of Sanskrit.

Some Hindus believe there is one universal God, Brahma, who takes on the forms of many gods and goddesses. Other Hindus believe that each god and goddess is a deity in his or her own right, and should be worshipped individually. Some Hindus believe in **reincarnation**, meaning that the soul lives forever and will return again and again, living in different bodies, long after a person's death.

reincarnation (ree-in-kahr-NAY-shuhn) being born on Earth again in another body after dying

Most representations of Brahma, such as this fourteenth-century Thai statue, have four faces.

Today, more than ninety percent of the people in Thailand practice Buddhism.

Hindu Castes

The Vedic people who followed early Hinduism introduced the idea of a **caste**, or class, system, which is still followed in modern India today. According to the Vedas, the early Vedic people divided themselves into two classes, the *arya* and the *daha*. These two classes eventually evolved into a three-class division of society: priests, warriors, and commoners.

By about 1000 BCE, the Vedics had created four distinct classes of people in their society, known as the *caturvarnas*, or "four colors." The highest caste was the Brahman priests, who were the religious leaders, teachers, and philosophers. Next were the nobles or warriors, known as the Kshatriya. Merchants, farmers, and craftspeople known as Vaishya followed. Unskilled laborers and servants were the *shudra*. A fifth group of people were below the shudras. These people were literally outcasts, part of a group outside of the caste system.

caste (KAST) one of the hereditary social classes in Hindu society

Buddhism

In the sixth century BCE, an Indian prince named Siddhartha Gautama was unhappy. He felt something was missing from his life, despite being surrounded by the riches and splendor of royalty. In about 538 BCE, when he was around twenty-five years old, he left the comfort of his wealth and began to travel, searching for spiritual guidance. Legends say that one day, while sitting under a Bodhi, a type of fig tree, he received enlightenment and came to understand the meaning of life. There he became Buddha, or the "enlightened one."

What came to him under the tree was the idea of the Four Noble Truths. The first is that life means suffering. Second, desiring things such as money, pleasure, people, professions, or power causes suffering. The third noble truth is that a person can end suffering by ending the desire to have worldly things. The final truth is the instruction on how to let go of wants and desires to find enlightenment.

Bodh Gaya is the home of the famous Mahabodhi Temple.

Today, millions of Buddhist pilgrims journey to Bodh Gaya in northeastern India to visit the Bodhi tree where Buddha received enlightenment. The tree that stands today is a descendant of the original tree, and Buddhist temples and monasteries surround it. In modern times, it is the custom to plant a Bodhi tree in every Buddhist monastery.

Buddha devoted the rest of his life to teaching others how to achieve the same enlightenment he had found. Buddha taught that each person, not the gods, controlled his or her own destiny. This was a new way of practicing religion in the ancient world, and people embraced this way of thinking. By the time Buddha died around 483 BCE, a small group of his followers had developed in the Gangetic Valley.

The Mauryan emperor Ashoka gave the first official attention to the ideas and faith of Buddhism. After the Battle of Kalinga in 262 BCE, Ashoka devoted his life to the teachings of Buddha and promoted peace throughout his empire. Ashoka also sent missionaries throughout India and into foreign kingdoms such as Egypt, Palestine, and Greece to preach the teachings of Buddhism.

ARCHITECTURE, ART, AND SCULPTURE IN ANCIENT INDIA

Each era of Indian history had its unique culture and art forms, from the civilizations of the Indus Valley, to the Vedas written by the Vedic nomads, to the glory of the Ajanta Caves of the Gupta Empire.

There are few notable examples of art from the Indus Valley culture, but one famous sculpture stands out above the rest. Scholars call the figure, which was found at Mohenjo Daro, "dancing girl." It is a slender bronze sculpture of a young woman wearing bangles and jewels. Another object, the Mehi mirror, has a copper handle shaped like a female figure, so that the person who looks into the mirror becomes the figure's face.

Huge statues of Buddha can be found at temples throughout the world.

Many small figurines found at Mauryan sites indicate the importance of art in that culture. Significant traces of Mauryan architecture have also survived, and they show expertly built structures, often decorated with elaborate carvings. Many of Ashoka's Rock Edict pillars are topped with carved lions, now the symbol of modern India. Ancient writers described golden pillars and statues in the Mauryan capital city of Pataliputra, but none have ever been found.

From about 120 BCE to 200 CE, ancient Indians carved temples out of solid rock. Many of these extraordinary structures can be found in caves on the Deccan Plateau. These rock-cut temples and chambers were not only places of worship. They also provided safe lodging for travelers, pilgrims, and traders. Temples carved into cliffs were naturally climate controlled, making them well suited for the extreme temperatures of the Deccan Plateau. They were cool in summer and comfortable in winter months.

One of the most impressive Deccan rock-cut temples is found in the Karla Caves. It is one of the oldest Buddhist rock-cut temples in India. Its soaring columns, horseshoe-shaped windows, and arched ceilings are a marvel of ancient architecture. Today, it is still a place of worship for Hindus and Buddhists.

GUPTA EMPIRE: INDIA'S GOLDEN AGE OF ACHIEVEMENT

When people around the world imagine ancient Indian achievements, it is likely that they're thinking of the Gupta period. During this time, incredible accomplishments were made in art, architecture, literature, and sculpture. Artists and learned people enjoyed a high status in Gupta culture, and the government encouraged their work by paying them salaries.

About 255 miles (410 km) northeast of modern Mumbai are the caves of Ajanta. These Buddhist rock-cut caves were carved between the second century BCE and the fifth century CE. They are filled with remarkably beautiful and complex paintings and sculptures of the Gupta period. Most of the wall paintings are crowded with colorful, vibrant figures in such lifelike poses that it seems as if they might actually be moving. The artwork illustrates stories called *jatakas*, which are tales about the previous lives of Buddha, in human and animal form. Others depict events from the life of the real Buddha and show details about daily life in ancient India.

The temple in the Karla Caves was created during the first century BCE.

Beautiful paintings decorate the walls of the Ajanta Caves.

stupas (STOO-pahz) moundlike structures containing Buddhist holy objects, used by Buddhists as places of worship

salvation (sal-VAY-shuhn) the state of being saved from sin, evil, harm, or destruction

Gupta-era places of worship also included **stupas**, or domelike temples. Stupas symbolize the achievement of Nirvana—the release of the soul from this world into **salvation**. The earliest stupas were built to house relics of Buddha, including his ashes. When Ashoka converted to Buddhism, he had all the original stupas opened and the ashes distributed to the thousands of stupas he built. The Great Stupa at Sanchi in Madhya Pradesh, central India, was commissioned by Ashoka, but greatly embellished and enlarged in the following centuries. The Mirpur Khas Stupa, built in the fourth century CE, featured a number of complex arches, indicating that the Indians were already skilled arch makers. The Dhamek Stupa was built in about 500 CE and is said to be the first place that Buddha gave a sermon after he received his enlightenment of the Four Noble Truths. In the mid-seventh century CE, it is believed that the Dhamek Stupa stood 300 feet (91 m) high and was home to fifteen hundred priests.

Gupta temple architecture also featured freestanding temples made of permanent materials such as brick and stone. The stone temple of Dasavatara in Deogarh in central India is dedicated to the Hindu god Vishnu. It features intricate wall carvings depicting several aspects of Vishnu's life and numerous Hindu deities. Parvati Temple, also in central India, is another classic example of Gupta-era architecture. It is dedicated to the goddess Parvati, Vishnu's wife.

The gates leading to the Great Stupa at Sanchi were carved in the 1st century CE with intricate images from the Jatakas, stories of the past Buddhas.

The Dasavatara Temple was built in the sixth century CE.

The Gandhara school of art and sculpture was the main style of art in Gupta-era India. Artists often took inspiration from Hindu gods and goddesses. They mixed these influences with old Buddhist folktales and philosophy to create a unique Buddhist art form. Most sculpture focuses on religious Buddhist themes, with the dominant form being the standing or seated Buddha. The seated Buddha is usually depicted cross-legged, a familiar image to modern people. The figures in Gandhara works, thousands of which have survived, were balanced and well proportioned. The figures were often depicted with fanciful gestures and postures.

HIGHER EDUCATION DURING THE GUPTA PERIOD

Some of the first universities in the world were established during the Gupta Empire, and students from around the world came to India to study. Some universities focused on specific subjects. Opened in about 700 BCE, Takshila, in present-day Pakistan, specialized in medicine. The school at Vallabhi, in western India, focused on Buddhist learning. Other schools of higher learning included Ujjain, for the study of astronomy; Ajanta, for art and architecture; and Sarnath, for Buddhism.

THE FIRST GLOBAL UNIVERSITY

The university at Nalanda, in northeastern India, was one of the major centers of higher education in the ancient world. Built in the fifth or sixth century CE, the university was an important educational resource until its destruction by Muslim invaders in about 1193. The school focused mainly on Buddhist studies, but it also trained students in fine arts, medicine, mathematics, astronomy, politics, and the art of war.

Each student's food, lodging, and education were free. They were paid for by donations from local villages and the government. Students, however, had to pass a difficult exam to be admitted to the university. Only about three out of every ten students made the grade. Students lived, worked, and studied in a complex that included eight separate compounds, ten temples, meditation halls, a large dining hall, and lecture halls. The lush grounds included lakes and parks. The library was nine stories tall and held thousands of documents. Monks spent their days in the library copying books so that scholars could have their own collections.

Nalanda was one of the world's first universities.

The campus included dormitories—the first ever created—that housed up to ten thousand students from places as diverse as Korea, Japan, China, Tibet, Indonesia, Persia, and Turkey. More than two thousand teachers and scholars also lived at the school. Studying at Nalanda was a great honor, although students were not awarded with a degree, nor was there any specific amount of study time required.

Today, there are plans to rebuild the great university into a modern international school for Buddhist teachings. Countries around the world are contributing to the construction of a new university near the ruins of the ancient school.

Students traveled great distances to study at Nalanda.

SCIENTIFIC LEARNING IN THE ANCIENT WORLD

The ancient Indians made remarkable advances in sciences such as engineering, astronomy, mathematics, medicine, and language. The cities of Mohenjo Daro and Harappa are filled with advanced architecture, complete with elaborate citywide drainage systems with covered sewers. Both cities are laid out in precise grids, showing that the architects had training in mathematics and geometry concepts. Harappan culture was likely the first to develop a system of weights and measurements, and they were the first culture to use a form of the decimal system. The people of Harappa also developed new techniques in metalworking and produced copper, bronze, lead, and tin.

The Vedic peoples had an understanding of astronomy and the cosmos. Several passages in the Vedas describe calculating the dates of sacrifices and rituals based on the movement of heavenly bodies. The Shulba Sutras, additions to the Vedas, discuss the cardinal directions of north, west, south, and east as helpful when building religious altars.

The Gupta-era astronomer Aryabhata the Elder, born in 476 CE, was one of India's greatest scientific thinkers. Aryabhata was the first to understand that eclipses were shadows cast by and cast upon Earth, rather than by the gods. He argued that Earth rotated on its axis daily and that the seeming movement of the stars was caused by Earth's rotation, not that the sky rotated, as people commonly believed. He also was the first to calculate the exact length of a year, and made important studies in algebra and trigonometry.

MEDICINE

Although Indian cultures practiced many different systems of medicine through the ages, only a small number survive to this day.

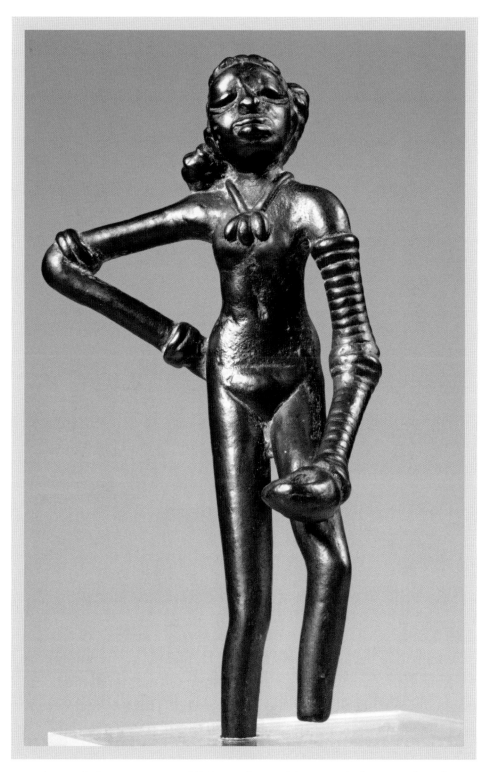

Ancient Indian artisans were skilled at working with bronze and other types of metal.

A statue of Aryabhata stands at the Inter-University Centre for Astronomy and Astrophysics in Pune, India.

The most popular is probably Ayurveda, meaning "the knowledge for long life." Ayurveda is a Hindu system of traditional medicine originally practiced during the Vedic period. This medical system is outlined in two Sanskrit texts, the *Sushruta Samhita* and the *Charaka Samhita*, written between 200 BCE and 100 BCE.

The *Charaka* is divided into 120 chapters and includes sections on drugs, food, diseases and their treatment and prevention, human anatomy, and much more. The text also describes surgery as the most useful part of medical training and discusses how to perform eye surgery, remove splinters and arrows, and even perform simple plastic surgery. The *Sushruta*, named for an ancient Indian surgeon, discusses more than 1,000 illnesses and plant and animal preparations used to treat them.

Today, Ayurveda is still practiced in many places around the world, including the United States and India, although many of its remedies and procedures have not been scientifically tested for their safety or health benefits.

Ayurveda remains a popular practice in many parts of the world.

CHAPTER SIX

THE PATH TO INDEPENDENCE

The invasion of the Huns and the decline of the Gupta Empire in the fifth century CE marked the beginning of a new era in ancient Indian history. India, which had been relatively free of foreign intervention for many hundreds of years, became the object of conquest for invading armies.

In the early eighth century CE, bands of Muslim warriors from West Asia began invading the region of modern-day Pakistan, which was then part of India. The Muslims came to spread their religion, Islam, which had been founded by the prophet Muhammad about one hundred years earlier. For hundreds of years, Muslim groups waged wars against India's population. They destroyed temples in order to take control of their land and resources.

In the beginning of the thirteenth century, another wave of Muslim peoples invaded India, this time from Persia, Turkey, and Afghanistan. Called the Mamluks, they occupied Delhi in the Indo-Gangetic Plain and established dynasties that ruled for more than three hundred years. These rulers had better relationships with the Hindu population, allowing them to practice their religion, rather than forcing them to accept Islam. However, many Hindus converted to Islam during these years.

Mamluk dynasties soon weakened, and rebellions and civil wars broke out as various regions of India fought for their independence. In about 1350, southern India claimed its independence as a Hindu state. The people of the Deccan became independent as an Islamic state.

A final invasion of Muslims came from central Asia in the early sixteenth century. Led by Babur, the Muslim armies crushed all Muslim and Hindu resistance. Babur founded the mighty Mughal Empire, the most powerful dynasty in Indian history, which ruled India for about two hundred years. Under the third Mughal emperor, Akbar the Great, Hindus enjoyed religious freedom and were welcomed as court advisers and leading military commanders.

After taking over India, the Mamluks built many mosques.

Akbar the Great reigned from 1556 until 1605.

Europeans were the next to cast their attentions on India. Beginning in the early sixteenth century, European nations began setting up trading posts in port cities on India's west coast. In time, the Portuguese, Dutch, English, and French established a thriving network of trade to and from India.

The British established dominance through the East India Company, a business that traded in many Indian goods, especially cotton, silk, tea, and salt. In 1757, the company's armies defeated the French-supported Muslim ruler of Bengal, which gave Britain control of trade in the region and won them territories and some political power. In 1764, the company defeated a Mughal army and gained political control of Bengal. By the mid-nineteenth century, the company controlled most of India, politically and economically.

In 1857, Hindu and Muslim soldiers serving in the East India Company's army rebelled against their British Christian officers. The soldiers believed that the British were trying to convert them and force them to do things their religions did not allow. The British brutally put down the rebellion, and power in India was transferred from the East India Company to the British Crown, thus becoming part of the British Empire.

The Past Is Present

ANCIENT INDIA'S UNIDENTIFIED FLYING OBJECTS?

The Sanskrit word *vimana* has several different meanings, including "palace," "temple," and "flying machines" as described in ancient Indian texts. The Vedas describe flying chariots pulled by horses and used by various Hindu deities. The Rig Veda, the oldest Vedas writing, mentions a flying craft that can be interpreted as a "mechanical bird." Some Sanskrit texts describe gods waging battles in engine-powered vimanas equipped with deadly weapons similar to modern-day lasers or Star Wars–like death rays. Today, some people believe the ancient astronaut theory, which claims aliens have been visiting Earth for thousands of years. Believers point to the ancient Indian accounts of vimanas as proof that ancient peoples have had contact with UFOs and extraterrestrial beings. However, this theory is not accepted by serious scholars.

British rule in the subcontinent was called the British Raj and would last from 1858 to 1947, the year India gained its independence from Britain. The independence movement was largely led by Mohandas Gandhi, the Hindu son of a government official. Trained as a lawyer, Gandhi successfully opposed British rule with nonviolent methods such as economic boycotts and civil disobedience.

The prospect of an independent nation led by the Hindu majority did not please India's Muslim population. After centuries of tensions between the two groups, the Muslims still mistrusted the Hindus—even as much as they mistrusted the British Raj. The British agreed to leave India to the Indians, and in August 1947 they formally established two separate self-governing nations: the Union of India for the Hindus and the Dominion of Pakistan for the Muslims. Since 1947, the two countries have fought several wars and numerous skirmishes along their common border.

The story of ancient India is the chronicle of many cultures and civilizations rising and falling over thousands of years. Each time, much was lost. But more survived and lived on to influence the cultures that came afterward. Much of modern India's life, religions, science, technology, and culture have come directly from those ancient people. Often there is no separation of ancient from modern.

Overall, information about India's earliest ancient cultures is difficult to find. Few contemporary written accounts of these civilizations have survived, and many ancient writings have never been deciphered. We've been able to learn much, however, from ancient religious texts that offer glimpses into how Indian societies lived. Beautiful carvings, statues, and artwork provide a look at how the ancients viewed their society and their religions.

Mohandas Gandhi helped lead the struggle for India's independence.

Each Indian culture had a period of dominance, followed by a decline. The Indus Valley people likely watched as their landscape and environment slowly collapsed, leaving dry riverbeds where life-giving water once flowed and dusty fields where fertile land had thrived. The Mauryan Empire, the first great ancient Indian empire, crumbled from the inside, a victim of weak rulers who were unable to fight back foreign invaders. The Gupta Empire, vast and powerful, was no match for wave after wave of outside armies that relentlessly attacked until the empire was destroyed.

The disappearance of each culture, however, did not signal the loss of that culture's great achievements. The religions of Hinduism and Buddhism, for instance, evolved and moved forward with the new cultures that came after. Scientific knowledge that began in ancient India—mathematical concepts, and ideas about astronomy and medicine—spread to the rest of the world and became the foundation for new discoveries. The art, sculpture, and literature of the ancient Indians survived through the centuries, becoming just as much a part of modern Indian culture as they were when they were created.

Thanks to discoveries like this at such sites as Mohenjo Daro, we have knowledge of the Indus Valley civilizations.

Modern India is a vibrant nation with a rich history.

BIOGRAPHIES

ALEXANDER THE GREAT (356–323 BCE) was a Greek military leader from Macedon who conquered much of the Eastern world from the Ionian Sea to the Himalayas. He was never defeated in battle and is considered one of history's most successful commanders.

ARYABHATA THE ELDER (476–CA. 550 CE) was one of ancient history's first great astronomers, discovering how eclipses occur and being the first to accurately calculate the length of a year.

ASHOKA (REIGNED 270–232 BCE), the greatest Mauryan king, gave up warfare after witnessing the horrors of his conquest of Kalinga. The Rock Edicts he erected throughout his empire provide us with important information about ancient Indian life, including how he ruled India by the Buddhist principles of nonviolence and harmony.

BUDDHA (CA. 563–CA. 483 BCE), born Siddhartha Gautama, gave up his royal heritage to search for spiritual enlightenment. His teachings provided the foundation for the Buddhist religion.

SIR JOHN **MARSHALL** (1876–1958 CE) was an English archaeologist whose excavations led to the discovery of Harappa and Mohenjo Daro. He also made important discoveries at Knossos, on the island of Crete in the Mediterranean Sea.

CHANDRAGUPTA **MAURYA** (REIGNED 321–297 BCE) was the founder of the Mauryan Empire. After the attacks of Alexander the Great, he conquered much of northern India.

MEGASTHENES (CA. 350–CA. 290 BCE) was a Greek ambassador to the court of Chandragupta Maurya and wrote of his experiences in a book called *Indica*. Although modern historians question the accuracy of much of what Megasthenes described, *Indica* is still considered one of the richest sources of Mauryan-era information.

JAMES **PRINSEP** (1799–1840 CE) was an English scholar who was employed in Calcutta, India, in the early nineteenth century. He was the first to decipher and translate Ashoka's Rock Edicts. After his death, the citizens of Calcutta built an archway, called Prinsep's Ghat, in his honor.

TIMELINE

2800 BCE:
Indus Valley civilization begins.

2600 BCE: *Harappa and
Mohenjo Daro flourish
as large metropolises.*

7000 BCE	3000 BCE	2500 BCE	2000 BCE

1800–1700 BCE:
*Indus Valley civilization
disappears.*

7000–3300 BCE:
*Mehrgarh culture
flourishes.*

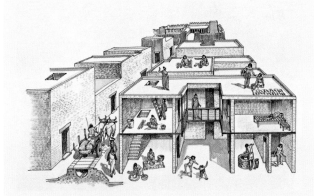

333 BCE:
Alexander the Great of Macedon defeats the Persian Empire.

500 BCE:
Vedic culture ends.

1200 BCE:
The Rig Veda is composed.

CA. **538 BCE:**
Buddha gains spiritual enlightenment.

1500 BCE   **1000 BCE**   **750 BCE**   **500 BCE**

326 BCE:
Alexander the Great attacks the northwestern provinces of India.

321 BCE:
Chandragupta Maurya becomes the ruler of north India.

270 BCE:
Ashoka the Great becomes king.

1500 BCE:
The earliest of the Vedas are created.

320 CE:
*Chandragupta I establishes
the Gupta Empire.*

CA. 376 CE:
*Chandragupta II becomes king and
begins the golden age of ancient India.*

476 CE:
*The astronomer
Aryabhata is born.*

480 CE:
*The Huns conquer most
of the Gupta Empire.*

CA. 184 BCE:
*The Mauryan
Empire collapses.*

0 CE   **500 CE**   **750 CE**

EARLY 8TH CENTURY CE:
*Muslims invade modern-
day Pakistan.*

550 CE:
*Vishnugupta, the last
Gupta ruler, dies.*

SECOND CENTURY BCE:
First paintings at Ajanta Caves are created.

232 BCE:
Ashoka dies.

262 BCE:
*Ashoka conquers Kalinga, regrets the
slaughter, and turns to Buddhism.*

EARLY 13TH CENTURY CE:
Mamluks occupy Delhi and rule the Indo-Gangetic Plain for three hundred years.

CA. 1350 CE:
Southern India claims independence from the Mamluks; Deccan becomes an independent state.

1857 CE:
Hindu and Muslim soldiers rebel against officers of the East India Company; the rebellion is brutally crushed.

1858–1947 CE:
British Raj rules India.

1947 CE:
Separate states of India and Pakistan are established.

1000 CE   **1500 CE**   **2000 CE**

1837 CE:
Englishman James Prinsep successfully deciphers Ashoka's Rock Edicts.

1764 CE:
Britain's East India Company gains political and economic control of Bengal.

EARLY 16TH CENTURY CE:
Babur founds the Mughal Empire, which rules India for two hundred years; Europeans establish trading outposts in India.

GLOSSARY

alliances (uh-LYE-uhn-sez) agreements to work together for some result

archaeologists (ahr-kee-AH-luh-jists) people who study the past, which often involves digging up old buildings, objects, and bones and examining them carefully

caste (KAST) one of the hereditary social classes in Hindu society

civilization (siv-uh-li-ZAY-shun) a developed and organized society

clans (KLANZ) large groups of families descended from a common ancestor

deciphered (di-SYE-fuhrd) figured out something that is written in code or is hard to understand

dynasty (DYE-nuh-stee) series of rulers belonging to the same family

edicts (EE-dikts) orders issued by a person in authority

excavations (ek-skuh-VAY-shunz) holes dug in the earth to search for something buried, as in archaeological research

immortality (im-or-TAL-i-tee) the quality of never dying; living forever

loincloths (LOYN-klawths) garments worn around a man's waist

martial art (MAHR-shuhl AHRT) style of fighting or self-defense

missionaries (MISH-uh-ner-eez) people who are sent to a foreign land to teach about religion

monarchies (MAH-nur-keez) governments in which the head of state is a king or queen

monsoon (mahn-SOON) a rainy summer season brought on by strong winds from the ocean

nomads (NO-madz) members of a community who travel from place to place instead of living in the same place all the time

pillars (PIL-urz) columns that support part of a building or that stand alone as a monument

raja (RAH-jhah) a Vedic clan chieftain

reincarnation (ree-in-kahr-NAY-shuhn) being born on Earth again in another body after dying

salvation (sal-VAY-shuhn) the state of being saved from sin, evil, harm, or destruction

scribes (SKRIBZ) people who copy books, letters, contracts, and other documents by hand

stupas (STOO-pahz) moundlike structures containing Buddhist holy objects, used by Buddhists as places of worship

subcontinent (sub-KAHN-tuh-nuhnt) a large landmass, such as India, that is part of a continent but is considered geographically or politically an independent region

tribute (TRIB-yoot) something done, given, or said to show thanks or respect, or to repay an obligation

vish (VISH) Vedic clans or tribes

FIND OUT MORE

BOOKS

Dalal, Anita. *Ancient India: Archaeology Unlocks the Secrets of India's Past*. Washington, DC: National Geographic, 2007.

Richardson, Hazel. *Life in the Ancient Indus River Valley*. New York: Crabtree Publishing, 2005.

Schomp, Virginia. *Ancient India*. New York: Marshall Cavendish Benchmark, 2010.

Visit this Scholastic Web site for more information on Ancient India:
www.factsfornow.scholastic.com
Enter the keywords **Ancient India**

INDEX

Page numbers in *italics* indicate a photograph or map.

ABOUT THE AUTHOR

Allison Lassieur has written more than eighty books about history, world cultures, ancient civilizations, science, and current events. She lives with her husband in Tennessee.